Salvation and Damnation

Kyle Parton
April Twelfth
Two thousand four

Written as a final paper for credit in
Rel234 - Doctrine of Salvation & Holiness
with Dr. Chris Bounds,
Indiana Wesleyan University

Presented the winter of 2005 at the
IWU Philosophy Club

Published by Epiphany Publishing, LLC
www.epiphanypublishing.us

ISMB: 978-0-692-48012-0

INTRODUCTION

"No facts are to me sacred; none are profane;
I simply experiment, an endless seeker with no Past at my back."
-Ralph Waldo Emerson

The last few dozen months have been a very complicated season in my life. I think of it as the proverbial "quarter-life crisis." Through the process of (1) truly beginning to understand why modernity is breathing its last few pathetic breaths on life-support (optimistically speaking), (2) watching the calling and purpose I thought I had slowly combust into a caustic heap of naïve evangelical trash, (3) having the stereotypical struggles that a young philosopher is prone to having and (4) dealing with a good amount of classic existential angst, I can say that I have had more than a few theological complications. When I "lost my modernity," I lost my entire God-concept with it. As a result, the ensuing anger, skepticism and angst that I have experienced have left me mere nanometers away from losing my faith.

With this in mind, know that the speculations and observations that I have tried to systematically present regarding the concept of salvation and damnation are neither orthodox nor evangelical. As you read on, you will come to observe that I believe in mystery. I believe that we *know* nothing with certitude. I believe that we should realize that we are not enlightened. I believe that in questioning our faith we can skim away that which is empty doctrinal language and in its place discover that which is earnestly meaningful. The irony of doubt is this: sometimes it is only in losing our certainty that we gain true sincerity. And in this there is a subsequent humility that I hope you find in these few pages of reflection. As Denis Diderot (1713-84) once said, "What has not been examined impartially has not been well examined. Skepticism is therefore the first step toward truth." At this point in my salvation, I do not care if my beliefs are educated, rational or orthodox. What I care about is that I do have beliefs, and while they may not be true, they are sincere.

My final disclaimer is this: know that I am an infallibilitst at best. I believe we can use the Bible as a tool to help us begin to know more about God; but I do not believe it is the theological textbook that we often assume it to be. God speaks through the Bible; but it seems that God can speak through any ass that is willing to be used (Num. 22.28). I have tried to stay within a reasonably Biblical parameter when it comes to the larger issues addressed herein. But where the Bible is silent, I do my best to bite my tongue. While I will forever be on the side of philosophy anytime theology and philosophy have a methodological power-struggle, I have made myself begin to rationally surrender to the beautifully divine enigma anytime it manifests within the scriptures. And at this point, I have nothing to lose.

As is my custom as an author, I have deliberately constructed several subtle logical fallacies and cryptically hidden them in my reasoning throughout this work. Find one and I'll give you a sticker. Find two and I'll give you a cookie. Three? A smooch.

1

I ANTHROPOLOGY:
WHERE ATHANASIUS CHANGES THE SUBJECT

"Creation is not a sin, creation is not evil (as the Ascenders, the Gnostics, the Manichaeists, the Tharavadins would all maintain) – creation is not a sin, getting lost in creation is. For that point, the creatures that express the final perfection of Spirit now merely become the shadows in the Cave obscuring Spirit."
-Ken Wilbur

"You can live a lifetime and, at the end of it, know more about other people than you know about yourself."
-Beryl Markham

To begin, let the object of our theological inquiry be that which is in the mirror. As we will be asking several questions that deal with the nature of man, perhaps it is sensible to start off by making a few observations about the ego. What is the ego? Where does the incorporeal component of our being originate from? What does it mean to be made in the image and likeness of God?

The Nature of the Ego

Ego is Latin for "I." Even though the term is usually thought of in its Freudian connotations, we can use it to describe the subject of our reflection here, which is this: What are the ontological components of a man? What sentient entity is cogitating when one mentally processes or contemplates something? What is the nature of the being that is narrating when one says "I am lonely?" Simply put, what is the "I?"

Among other religions there is an incredibly wide scope of responses to these questions. While a Zoroastrian or Muslim would answer these questions similarly, an Orthodox Jew or Daoist would have a completely different answer. Buddhists understand the "I" to be a small collection of experience-generating manifestations of consciousness, or *skandhas*. These *skandhas*, when bonded together by desire, constitute the entity understood to be the "I." In Buddhist thought, there is no ego. However, within the scope of Christian thought there seems to be three prevailing answers to these questions, each of which has a historically sizeable number of advocates. These schools of thought are categorized as *trichotomism*, *dichotomism* and *monism*.

Trichotomism is the school of thought that is more popular in the Eastern Church. In this understanding of the ego, it is thought that there are three equally distinct constituents of the nature of man – body, soul and spirit. The scriptures that appear to advocate this understanding are mostly from the New Testament, such as 1 Thes. 5.23, Heb. 4.12 and 1 Cor. 14.14. Regarding the origin of this anthropology, Louis Berkhof's astute observations are worthy of note:

> The tripartite conception of man originated in Greek philosophy, which conceived of the relation of the body and the spirit of man to each other after the analogy of the mutual relation between the material universe and God. It was thought that, just as the latter could enter into communion with each other only by means of a third substance

3

or an intermediate being, so the former could enter into mutual vital relationships only by means of a third or intermediate element, namely the soul.[1]

Where trichotomists advocate a three-fold nature of man, dichotomists only acknowledge two by maintaining the same basic concept of the body but referring to the soul and spirit as one entity. Dichotomists, too, have scriptures to back up their position (such as Ecc. 12.7, Mt. 10.28 and Lk. 12.10). The other main school of thought that is notable among the history of Christian anthropology is monism. This Hebraic anthropology claims there to be no distinction between the body and soul/spirit (therefore implying the impossibility of a bodily resurrection). Due to the severity of this implication, we will not spend time here discussing this view as a legitimately orthodox anthropology.

A very difficult task when dealing with these anthropologies is in defining a clear ontological distinction between all the possible constituents of the ego. The body, or the somatic manifestation of the ego, is the easiest to define and understand of all the components. In labeling this part of man's being, I will use the Hindu term *jiva*, which they use to refer to the physical, empirical body. Unfortunately, even trichotomists often disagree regarding where the soul and spirit are mutually exclusive. Stanley Grenz describes the difference in this fashion: "Trichotomists see the 'spirit' as that part of a human being which is capable of knowing God. The 'soul,' in contrast, is the seat of the personality. Thus, it encompasses our intellect, emotions, and will."[2] A dichotomist has a much easier time categorizing these components by only distinguishing between the *jiva* and…well, everything else.

While there are frequent and diverse Biblical accounts of the reality, sentience and immortality of the soul/spirit, the Bible is inconveniently ambiguous in regard to the ontological details of the incorporeal essence of one's being. In addressing the concept of immateriality, Robert Landis observes:

> The *idea* philosophically associated with the term is of modern origin, (for the ancient philosophers seemed to have no conception of it,) and was originated as an offset to the debasing material philosophy of Hobbes, Toland, and others. It is in no way required, however, in an investigation of the subject before us. *Corruptibility* and *incorruptibility* convey ideas which are not beyond our reach. But the same cannot be said of *materiality* and *immateriality* in their professedly philosophical sense.[3]

It is at this point that we must note two problems with the anthropological approach of trichotomism, one of which demonstrates a profound ontological fallacy that is frequently committed by theologians and philosophers alike, and the other entails the linguistic nuances we improperly employ when speaking of our ego.

The first problem we will address is in regard to how we think of the distinguishability between incorporeal realities. Though our popular Western, philosophic concepts of time/space have been so deeply influenced by Einstein's relativity theory, the theological enterprise has been very slow to catch up with this ethos. There are countless doctrines that refer to incorporeal realities with terms that are only applicable to corporeal

[1] Berkhof, *Systematic Theology*, p. 191.
[2] Grenz, *Theology for the Community of God*, p. 203.
[3] Landis, *The Immortality of the Soul*, p. 40.

4

reality. Examples of this are prevalent in our eschatologies, anthropologies and other minute theological constructs, like…oh, say the Trinity.

Perhaps it is irony that the ontological fallacy we so frequently commit has unnecessarily complicated our doctrine for centuries. But where we have gone wrong when contemplating the incorporeal is completely understandable. We cannot be blamed for relating all other metaphysical realities to the simple logical analogies we know in our particular ontological sphere – the spatiotemporal. It is not our fault that the only metaphors we can construct are, at some point, contingent upon analogy to the physical laws of the spatiotemporal. But because of this, we have severe problems understanding a reality that does not necessarily have to be bound by the law of non-contradiction, such as the Trinity, Heaven/Hell, angels or the soul/spirit. The fallacy here is novel: we take the laws of physics that apply to our empirical reality and project (in the Freudian sense of the word) them onto all other incorporeal spheres of existence. In the case of the nature of the ego, the result is an unnecessarily dark line drawn between the soul and the spirit. If we are to be consistent in thinking of an incorporeal component of the ego as not being composed of matter, then we must therefore acknowledge that it cannot have two distinct parts, for these quantifying terms only refer to material realities. Perhaps we could refer to this fallacy as *spatiotemporal projection*. Keep your eyes open for it. It's popular.

The second problem we must address is in the erroneous reference to the incorporeal component of the ego as *eternal*. As we become more and more familiar with the concept of eternity, we can begin to become rationally comfortable with the idea of infinite duration of existence (or something having no end); however, it will be forever impossible for our minds to be comfortable with the idea of inceptionless existence (or something having no beginning), and for that matter, *preexistence*. I believe the reason for this is simple. It is severely difficult, if not impossible, to define the word *eternity*. Today, the word is frequently used as a synonym for infinity; however, this is not the full scope of how the Biblical concept of the word can be employed. Although the word is Biblically used as a synonym for infinite, *eternity* (δε, αιδιον) entails beginningless existence as well as endless existence. This is an important detail to note because it is critical in understanding the nature of the ego. In staying consistent with the Biblical language, only God is eternal. Any created entity has an ontological inception, and thus cannot be thought of as eternal. It is in this observation that I understand why our minds have the capacity to imagine infinity, but not inceptionless existence. We can understand infinity *because our ego is infinite*; in the same way, we cannot comprehend inceptionless existence *because our ego is not inceptionless*. It would seem that our minds are bound within the sphere of our ontological essence. We cannot comprehend something that completely transcends our being. I do not believe that this is bad news. Without sounding too Neo-Platonic, I take great security in the concept of God as the Great Transfinite Mystery. It simply means that we must use caution when using these ontological labels in reference to the ego.

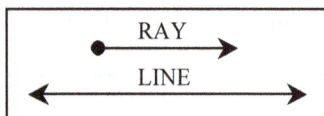

I would propose that we consider this anthropological issue in this way: the nature of man's ego can be effectively likened to the mathematical *ray*. There is a definite point of emergence, or ontological inception, and infinite continuation. Contradistinctively, God's ego (if I may use the term very loosely) can be more likened to the mathematical *line* - no beginning, no end. While our ego is not eternal, it is infinite. And although all mankind has a similar ontogenesis, the Bible is relatively clear that some component of our being will infinitely exist, whether in Heaven or Hell.[4]

To summarize, I feel that I can Biblically affirm the existence of an incorporeal essence, and I feel that I can make a satisfactory assertion that the Biblical soul/spirit is, in actuality, the ego. But that is about the extent of any description or speculation I can safely make about the nature of the ego. Because the Bible contains no ample description regarding the nature of the "I" and because we cannot use consistent or accurate language to construct an analogy to describe it, I am again lead to the conclusion that we must stand in reverent silence at the brilliant mystery of God's creation. We will never be aware of the exact nature of our ego. Such things are too wonderful for us to know.

The Origen of the Ego

Can we identity the manner in which the ego emerges into being? Historically, there are a few theories regarding this issue. The *creationism* view states that God creates a new soul for each person and sends it to that person's body sometime between conception and birth. The Biblical foundation for this view can be found in such scriptures as Ps. 127.3, Heb. 12.9, and Is. 42.5. Another popular view within the Church has been *traducianism*, which states that the soul as well as the body of each person is inherited from the person's mother and father at the time of conception. This idea can be found in Gen 1.24, 5.3 and Heb. 7.10. The third and most novel theory is called *pre-existentianism*, in which it is though that our souls exist in heaven long before our bodies are conceived in the wombs of our mommies. This view isn't particularly scriptural, but it is held by many Jewish mystics and Christendom's very own anomaly, Origen. Each of these views has its strengths, but I'm not so sure that we will ever be able to scientifically calculate the exact ontogenesis of our ego. Thankfully, it is not a critically important issue in the grand scope of our salvation.

The Imago Dei

The Bible frequently describes man as being made in the "image and likeness of God." (Gen. 1.26f, 5.1, 9.6 and James 3.9) What exactly does this mean? The historical views of the Church are, again, a bit open-ended, but there is great merit in examining these traditions of antiquity. Several Christians have understood this language to simply be Hebrew parallelism (meaning "image" and "likeness" poetically describe the same reality). The *substantive view* interprets this language to mean that the image and likeness of God is a real characteristic within the individual nature of humanity. This literal view has been held by many of the early Church fathers and other later figures, such as Luther and Calvin. Another Eastern school of thought that interprets this language differently is found in the *relational view*, which states that the image and likeness can be seen when we have a relationship with God and/or humanity. In essence, the image of God is the Church. This view has been held by such popular theologians as Emil Brunner and Karl Barth. The fourth popular view is the *functional view*, which understands image and likeness in terms of what humans do. Held by Norman Snaith and

---

[4] Note the *spatiotemporal projection*. There's a free one.

Leonard Verduin, this view maintains that we resemble God when we actively exercise dominion over the Earth.

Despite the variety in these views, we can understand the image and likeness (in the broadest sense) to mean this: because we are the only element of creation bearing this label, we are similar to God in a way that is unique to all creation. This aspect of the ego's identity sets us apart from all other objects or beings that exist. I believe we are safe in understanding this to be in reference to the all components of our being – incorporeal or somatic. The implications of this will be discussed later.

II PATHOLOGICAL HAMARTIOLOGY

"All sin tends to be addictive,
and the terminal point of addiction is what is called damnation."
-Wystan Hugh Auden

"There ain't no sin and there ain't no virtue. There's just stuff people do. It's all part of the same thing. And
some of the things folks do is nice, and some ain't nice, but that's as far as any man got a right to say."
-John Ernst Steinbeck

In the last two or three months, I have learned many painful, firsthand lessons about what computer viruses can do and how hard they can be to remove if you happened to delete your antivirus software in a moment of profound stupidity. At the time of writing this, the Symantec™ Online Virus Encyclopedia contained 26,294 detections of individual viruses, worms and Trojan horses that exist online – just waiting to make a warm nest out of your hard drive. My poor laptop has been losing a battle to several Trojan horses for some time now. A Trojan horse is something that appears to be a legitimately safe file, but is actually a harmful program that can seriously affect a computer by stealing or destroying data. What makes a Trojan horse different from a virus or a worm is in the way it is spread. Unlike viruses or worms, one actually has to open or download the program in order for a Trojan horse to spread. In this regard, the virtual-pathology of Trojan horses is unique in a way that will serve to provide an example of our hamartiological analogy.

Several weeks back I had a moment of naïve and curiously explorative stupidity and decided to open an email attachment from a "gradschool" that I had expressed interest in. Subsequently, the Trojan horse that I downloaded proceeded to settle in and wait for the right opportunity to release and install all the worms that came – free of charge – with the viral attachment. Just the other morning, in reflecting upon this, I realized that somewhere out in the world, there is a very intelligent person or group of people who spent a great amount of time writing code and designing the details of this program with one goal in mind: to find subtle ways of getting me to mistake the bad for good and thus let my guard down. When this has happened, their end has been achieved as I have welcomed this foreign, corrupting, malicious entity into my system. In this scenario I want to draw a hamartiological analogy to answer these questions: How did sin originate? What are the effects of original sin? What is the essence of our sin-nature?

Original Sin

If we are going to inquire about the origin of sin, we should, at some point, realize that sin did not enter the Kosmos through mankind. It is easy to think of the early Genesis accounts as a narrative describing how sin entered the world through Adam. While it is true that Adam is the first example of *humanity* succumbing to temptation, it is not true that Adam was the first *being* to sin. Despite Rom. 5.12, the Bible appears to indicate that sin was first found in the heart of Lucifer, which would have to have been prior to the Gen. 3 sin account. It is because Lucifer deviated from the will of God that sin/evil entered our reality. Taking notice of this, let us focus on humanity's hamartiological plight.

If the Bible is accurate in presenting the only way for man to be reconciled with his Creator, then the epic scenes in the opening chapters of Genesis contain the greatest moments of suspense and tragedy to ever occur in the existence of the Kosmos. I do not want to spend time debating if these chapters are figurative or parabolic. But one must realize that if the Genesis account of creation and the Fall is only poetic imagery, then we have no real substance from which to conjecture the origin of the Kosmos, good and evil, or mankind. This being said, I make my hamartiological speculations with the presupposition that these accounts have at least *some* literal truth to them.

In reading Genesis 1-3, we can point out several strange occurrences and many open ended questions. It is hard for our Greek-minded culture to come to grips with the fact that there are many important questions regarding the ontogenesis of the Kosmos for which the Bible simply has no satisfying answers. Even though any study of the creation account has a tendency to leave us with more questions than when we began, I believe it is worthwhile to spend some time investigating the plot-twists that occur there. The bottom line is that the Genesis narrative is too frustratingly indescriptive for us to gather detailed answers to most of the following questions.

First off, why did God decide to allow His beloved creation and Satan to coexist? After witnessing the destructive and persuasive power that Satan had upon the hosts of angels that followed him, how could He not deal with Satan before creating man? Could He not foresee that Satan would pursue man? Or could He at least have warned Adam that he might cross paths with this being? H. Orton Wiley proposes the idea that the garden was a probationary period in which man was supposed to choose to wholly glorify God by resisting temptation. God allowed temptation to occur because there was no other way to enable Adam's obedience to be evaluated and completed.

In reflecting upon this possibility, I have to humbly observe that in the state of affairs before the Fall, God already had obedience, fellowship, and intimacy with Adam. I have a really hard time rationalizing the idea that God would risk the wellbeing of His entire creation to attain something that was "more perfect" than what He Himself had created and instituted. The idea of a probationary period suggests that there is a degree of "perfection" attainable that is higher than the uncorrupted, sinless, and direct creation of God Himself. That man – right out of the box – was not whole. The fact that God categorically labeled his beloved work "Very good" and not "Almost complete" leads me to presume that God was conclusively pleased with the "level" of man's perfection. Furthermore, why isn't the idea of a probationary period even suggestively mentioned anywhere in scripture by Paul or someone else who had so much to say about Adam's sin? Karl Barth does a beautiful job describing the benefit, actualization, and justification inherent within creation as it was before the Fall:

> The only thing which can be better than what is by God (apart from God himself) is what is to develop out of what is in its communion and encounter with God. The only thing which can be better than creaturely existence is the goal of the covenant for which the creature is determined in and with its creation. But in the order of created existence as such there can be nothing better than what is. What is by God and is thus well pleasing to God, what is elected, accepted and justified by God, is for this reason not only good, but very good, perfect. Even the good and the best, which awaits its fulfillment at the goal of its fellowship and dealings with God, can add nothing to the

perfection of its being as such. Even its future glorification presupposes that it is already perfectly justified by the mere fact of its creation.[5]

The probationary view of the garden also presupposes that God would have removed Satan if Adam had resisted his ploys. Let us take a short detour and wonder: what would have happened to Satan if Adam had not sinned? Clearly, there are two possibilities: If Adam had resisted Satan's temptations and thus had not deviated from God in his heart, it seems sound to conjecture that God would have either dealt with Satan in some way or He would have let him continue to tempt Adam. But what do each of these possible courses of action imply?

Again, we can only speculate how God would have perhaps dealt with Satan's malevolence; however, I often entertain the idea that He would have somehow carried out one of more of the following options, in each of which we can find traces of our computer virus analogy: 1. Optimistically, I believe that God could have somehow taken steps to work out a means of redemption and grace for Satan and the fallen angels. Had this been the case, I believe that Christ could have "incarnated" to their ontological disposition in order to establish a salvific avenue in the same way that He was somatically incarnated into humanity's substance. This is similar to repairing a file infected by a virus. 2. God could have removed Satan in a way that he would be unable to further interact with humanity. It is not a stretch of my mind to imagine that God, in His omnipotence, could have easily spoken forth another mode of being in which Satan could have easily been confined and thus isolated from God's obedient children. This is similar to quarantining an unreparably infected file. 3. God could have simply destroyed Satan. With but a divine syllable, He could have completely dealt with the abysmal complications of sin, death and suffering. This is similar to deleting an infected file. However, at this point I feel it would be appropriately considerate to note that God *intensely* loved Lucifer. The divine pain that occurred in the omniemotional heart of God as the result of his rebellion is probably impossible to ever understand or articulate. Let us keep this in mind as the underlying tone when we reflect upon the entire plot of the early Genesis narrative. In all likelihood, the reason that He did not destroy *us* for *our* iniquity is the same reason that He did not destroy Satan: perfect love and grace.

In turn, we can also speculate about the implications of God letting Satan continue to freely roam about the Kosmos and tempt Adam and his descendants in spite of their devoted resistance to his agenda. In this hypothetical state of affairs, could Satan's unrestrained autonomy possibly be thought of as a means of growth for man (in the sense of the probationary ideal of levels of perfection)? Perhaps with each time a son of man resisted deviance, there was another victory over sin that was achieved, and thus a further level of perfection was attained. Frankly, this does not appear to be a very fair deal to humanity. Are we to think of God as the type of uninvolved bystander that this scenario depicts Him to be? Is He neutral? Is His name Passive? Surely we can conclude that God would have taken direct action if Adam had brought the epic scenario in the midst of the garden to His attention and asked for guidance. I believe He would have responded passionately. But we must note that regardless of how we want to approach these speculations, we are left with several open ended questions – one of which is probably unanswerable: When did God plan on dealing with Satan?

---

[5] Barth, *Church Dogmatics*, p. 366.

I am not convinced that thinking of the garden as a probationary period is the best way we can understand the situation. While I cannot propose an explanation for the reason God allowed these events to occur in the garden, the issues we have discussed convince me that Wiley's idea of a probationary period doesn't satisfactorily explain it.

Secondly, I want to address some of the dialogues that take place in the Genesis account. From these dialogues we can raise the following questions: Is sin the cause of death? At what point did Adam actually sin? Did Adam have to sin?

Death is frequently understood as the result of Adam's sin. Seeing how this is pretty heavily supported in scripture, I am not going to disagree. However, I do believe that we must acknowledge the possibility that a form of death could and would have occurred before the Fall. I have two reasons for this: 1. The population mandate (Gen. 1.28) was given before Adam sinned, and 2. the dietary mandates (Gen. 1.29 and 2.16) were also given before the Fall.

In regard to the population mandate, it must be observed that God commanded Adam to populate the earth *before* death as we know it had allegedly entered the world. There is a very serious problem with this order of events: if Adam were to continue to procreate before somatic death existed, humanity would have overpopulated the planet within a hard-to-predict amount of time. Unless God was planning on the occurrence of sin, therefore death, entering the world, could it be argued that this was a serious lack of foresight on God's part? Aren't there other ways of understanding this scenario?

In regard to the dietary mandates, we would do well to note that the man and woman had to eat in order to sustain themselves. Twice God explains to them that they were to eat the fruit He provided for nourishment. This leads me to think that their bodies were, more or less, of a similar somatic constitution as ours are now. If the man was running with a deer and accidentally tripped, hit his head on a rock and rolled into a lake, would he not have drowned? If he stepped on a sharp stick, would he not have bled? A wise man named Dutch once taught us that anything that bleeds can die.[6]

In examining Gen 1 – 3, we can interpret the events in this manner: in Gen. 1.29 and 2.16-17 God gives the original dietary restrictions and repercussions – eating of the tree of knowledge would cause death. Also, they were apparently allowed to originally eat of the tree of life and "live forever," although it is unclear if they had done so. In 3.19 God's decree declares that man will now return to the dust from which he came as a result of his deviance. This would suggest that he was not doomed to this fate prior to sinning. In 3.22 the divine soliloquy makes it reasonably clear that they would not (from that point on) live forever.

While I will maintain that death – as we now know it – is the result of the Fall, these scenarios lead me to believe it is a legitimate option to think that humanity was susceptible to a less destructive form of "death" prior to the Fall. Could it be that original man would, at the end of a long life, undergo some ontological alteration that would free him from the restrictions of his *jiva* and thus account for these complications? I do not see a great problem imagining this to be the case.

And thirdly, at what specific point did sin occur? We see the crafty serpent make its appearance at the beginning of Gen. 3 and begin to speak to the woman. By means of seemingly honest inquiry, the serpent began to lead the woman to question what God had clearly and directly spoken to them both. Bonhoeffer notes:

---

[6] Sound familiar? If not, I'm not telling…

> What is the real evil in [Satan's] question? It is not that a question as such is asked. It is that this question already contains the wrong answer. It is that with this question the basic attitude of the creature toward the Creator comes under attack. It requires humankind to sit in judgment on God's word instead of simply listening to it and doing it.[7]

Wiley has done insightful work in addressing the question of when the shift from temptation to sin actually occurred. Did sin occur at the external action of consuming the fruit or did it occur at the internal contemplation of disobedience? From an Old Testament perspective we might be more prone to focus on the external disobedience; A New Testament view might focus more on the internal deviance. Unfortunately, the scriptures do not shed any light upon the details of when sin actually occurred, so the only real answer we can give this important question is that Adam sinned at some point between Gen. 3.6 and 3.7.

The Kosmic Effects of Original Sin

Were the man and the woman the only entities effected by original sin? The divine curses that follow Adam's sin make it clear that there were other material ramifications to their disobedience besides their bodies returning to the dust. In the paradisiacal settings that were instituted before the Fall, creation existed in a harmony that we will never again have the chance to observe. The Kosmic breakdown that resulted from the effects of Gen. 3.6 reaches deep into the being of every material object, sentient or insentient. In man, we have already speculated that another form of death resulted from Adam's ineptitude. We might also note that the image and likeness of God that we were originally endowed with was marred and destroyed. A similar observation can even be made of all other organic creation: at the point of sin – whether it was its contemplation, initiation, or execution – supernovas exploded, sharks became excited by blood, leaves withered, and matter generally changed for the worse. I believe that the results of this sin affected every component of anything that existed, then or now, for the worse.

The Sin-Nature of the Ego

It is a widely-held Christian belief that mankind universally suffers the effects of Adam's sin from conception. In describing our intrinsic propensity towards selfishness, the popular theological language we use is usually something like *sin-nature* or *inherited corruption*. There are a few different approaches to the details of this issue, and some great $10 theological terms come out of it. For instance, the *example view* states that Adam's sin was a very minor act of disobedience that affected only himself. This is in austere contrast to the *solidarity view*, which maintains that a solidarity exists between Adam and his race. In this view, there are two main theories that work with these presuppositions. The first, the *realist/natural headship theory*, states that because Adam somatically embodied the entire human race in a single, collective entity, all people are co-sinners with Adam. The repercussions of the sin that Adam committed were passed on biologically to his children. A different approach to this is found in the *represent-*

---

[7] Bonhoeffer, p. 108-109.

ative/federal headship theory. This theory states that the union between Adam and his posterity is due to the fact that God appointed him as the representative head of the human race. In this perspective, we bear the consequences of his sin, but not to the same degree of responsibility that he does.

Even as there may be some differences between the solidarity views, they have a common theme that unites them both: all mankind suffers from the imperceptive decisions that Adam (the man *and* the woman, for the woman was not named Eve until after the Fall) made in the garden. While I will agree that our desires, emotions, bodies, and relationship with God are negatively affected due to the relationship of sin and our being, I cannot find an adequate scriptural argument that maintains these negative changes to be present from the womb. Mankind does have a sin-nature; however, I do not see why it has to be necessarily passed on from birth. This is where our computer virus analogy can be helpful.

I believe there are two perfect examples in Adam and Christ to illustrate this view. First, consider Adam: as we have discussed, Adam was without sin before Genesis 3.6. After his selfish decision, the results of his sin stayed with him until he returned to the dust. In all actuality, I believe this to still be an appropriate anthropological paradigm regarding our sin-nature. A similar scenario can be found examining Christ's life (with a bit of a different result). Christ was born without sin. The difference here is that when faced with temptations to make selfish decisions (most likely before his formal temptation by Satan), He did not deviate from the will of God. The result of this is what we could expect: sin did not corrupt His desires, body, etc. Both Adam and Christ began their lives with a hamartiological *tabula rasa*, as I believe we do today. I do not believe that we have inherited guilt. I can still read Rom. 5.18-19 and understand the situation Paul is describing as this: we are *tempted* because of Adam's sin; we are not *guilty* because of it. I have yet to run across any scriptures that explicitly and categorically contradict this view.

Although there are a few scriptures that describe man as sinful from the womb, there are countless others that describe man as sinful from childhood. The difference is important. We may note this in Grudem's comments:

> Moreover, even before [David] was born, he had a sinful nature, for "in sin did my mother conceive me" (Ps. 51:5). Here is a strong statement of the inherent tendency to sin that attaches to our lives from the very beginning. A similar idea is affirmed in Psalm 58:3, "The wicked go astray from the womb, that err from their birth, speaking lies."[8]

Thanks Wayne.[9] Yes, there are 2 scriptural references to being sinful from conception, both of which are the poetic imagery of David. In his self abasement, David claims he was sinful at birth/conception in Ps. 51, and in a pejorative reference to the wicked, he says they lie and are wayward from birth/conception in Ps. 58. While there are no other scriptures to support this view, there are several others that make it clear that man is sinful from early *childhood*, rather than conception. For instance, in Genesis 8.21 the very words of God refer to man as sinful from the time of childhood, rather than from the

---

[8] Grudem, *Systematic Theology*, p. 496.

[9] This proves I'm conservative. I mean, all I have to do to be an evangelical is quote Grudem, right?

womb. Other scriptural support for this idea can be found in Gen. 6.5, Job 14.1, Jer. 17.9, Mk. 7.21-23, Rom 5.12-21 and Eph. 2.1-5.

If we are born with a blank slate in regard to sin, then why do we struggle so badly? Why do we sin? Obviously, we are still tempted today. But think back to the first selfish choice you made. Even though there is probably no way to remember making such a decision, I believe there is a point in each individual's life where they are first faced with a decision to sin or not. (When I refer to selfishness, I am not referring to an infant crying because it's hungry. I am not convinced that the infant really chooses to cry out of selfish motivation. Although I believe that an infant is sinless prior to responding to temptation, it's not the fact that an infant is incapable of discerning between right and wrong that would save him, as the usual doctrines of the age of accountability would argue. Rather, it's the fact that he doesn't have the capacity for *anything* at this point. It's not that he has the competence for intellectual activity without moral capacity; it is the fact that he is in a complete bankruptcy of voluntary intellectual activity. Just because we can observe his natural vital motions (using Hobbes' terms) doesn't mean that he is choosing to act them out. Only upon the development of voluntary motions could one begin to be held accountable for them.) I believe it is when we give in to temptation for the first time that we give an unconscious admittance to corruption, perversion, and death. From the time that sin gets its foot in the door, we can kiss all hopes of innocence, simplicity, and guiltlessness goodbye and say hello to egocentricism, confusion, and damnation. That is, until we embark upon our salvation.

To summarize, I want to again emphasize that a computer virus is not hard-wired into one's system. I am solely responsible for what has happened to my computer, whether I understood the repercussions or not. The same can be said of my individual sin nature. From the womb, I believe I had no sin-nature hard-wired into my being. Rather, there was some point in my tiny existence where I began making decisions that were wholly selfish. These choices didn't even necessarily have to be the result of direct Satanic temptation. The majority of these decisions were probably due to an even more abhorrent nature within man: the *monkey-see-monkey-do* phenomenon. Anyway, from that point in my decisions, the natural result of my selfishness began to change the way I thought, felt, what I wanted, and who I generally was. It was when I "downloaded" sin into my system that it began to run rampant within me. Now, when comparing this theory with other classical sin-nature theologies, the end result looks pretty much the same; but the difference is great in terms of our original nature, and these differences have implications regarding the nature of salvation, which we will now discuss.

III Soteriology
Note the Brevity. Note the Mystery.

"Nothing is static. Even the Mona Lisa is falling apart."
-Tyler Durden

"Human salvation lies in the hands of the creatively maladjusted."
-Martin Luther King, Jr.

I have an irrevocably deep respect for most Eastern religions, specifically Buddhism. Many of the Asian religions do not have what we would call a soteriology. Hinduism and Buddhism do not regard salvation as a theological component of their faith. These ancient religions use a word that is wholly foreign to the vapid, egocentric, Western mind. They use the beautiful term *dharma* when broadly referring to ones salvific path. The word cannot really be easily translated because it has so many meanings that most of us do not have comprehensive analogies for in the first place, and I understand it just enough to I know I can't describe it. So I won't. But the whole point of one of the understandings of this word is that "salvation" is a path, not an act or a destination. Salvation is an existence, not an event. It is my hope to here explain a more *dharmic* approach to salvation than we are used to hearing in contemporary soteriologies.

The Restoration of the Imago Dei

If you are still reading this paper at this point, then chances are you have heard the basic Gospel message. Sin is bad, God is Holy. Man likes sin, God likes man. God becomes man, man likes God. Then you go to heaven, or something to that effect. I believe we are all at different levels of awareness as to what is really involved in this process. And I believe that in thinking of salvation primarily as the means of "going to heaven" we have tragically cheapened what it means to have life abundant on this side of the pearly gates. We seem to believe that the words "conversion" and "salvation" are equivocally interchangeable. But I believe the work that God does – that which we might call salvation – has much, much more depth to it than simply giving us a golden ticket to Paradise signed by Jesus.

I believe salvation is the process by which God and man partner together to reverse the spiritual, social and ontological consequences of the Fall. It is the process of restoring the unity that existed prior to the Fall of Man. I think of it as the dynamic, organic restoration of the image of God (Col. 3.10), the progressive renewal of the likeness of our Creator. This understanding has more to it than simply the forgiveness of sins. It has to do with existing to the fullest capacity that God has enabled us to exist - Heaven *and* Earth.

Dynamic, not Binary

We are so often guilty of having a *binary soteriology*; we believe that if we have prayed the "sinner's prayer" at an altar, then God has done a complete, static, final work in our heart. All we have to do is confess with our mouth and believe in our heart and it's a done deal. Of course, if you do not take these steps of repentance, you are not saved. You're either saved or damned. Black or white. 1 or 0. Unfortunately, I was of this mind for years. It has only been in the last few months that I have started to understand that there is more that God can do in our lives then save our souls. I suspect that Christ focused on what can occur here, in this life, more than we give Him credit for. If our view of salvation could be more wholistic, it would also include the obedience that can occur in this life. Do not believe that God is done working in your heart at the moment of conversion – or for that matter, do not believe that He just started. The phenomenon of God and man partnering together to reverse the effects of the Fall is a process that can span through one's entire lifetime. Although there are important points of growth we may be able to point out along the way, I do not believe the whole process should be thought of as a bulleted, singular, binary event.

Tailored Salvation

Many theologians have proposed a specific *ordo salutis*, or way of salvation. In these outlines of the salvific process, we can observe points that represent specific changes made and steps taken towards becoming what God originally designed us to be. While I do believe we can retrospectively map out some of the progress we make with God in our salvation, I do not believe there is a formulaic, rigid paradigm regarding how each individual person is restored to the image of God. Because no two sin-natures are identical, I don't see how two *ordo saluti* can be alike. I believe the salvific process is, in some degree, subjectively tailored to each unique case of God and man's partnership. The point where the first steps of repentance were taken in my salvation may be in a very different place when compared to where they occur in someone else's. The implication of this is important: although God is infinitely transcendent, He is also immanent enough to be aware of our specific sin-tendencies and thus able to uniquely partner with us in addressing them. We do not need to have a detailed, dogmatic *ordo salutis* in order to believe this. As we will now look at those who had such doctrines, we might note that perhaps it is even better if we do not.

The Salvific Enigma

I love reading about some of the earliest history in soteriological development. The whole Pelagius/Augustine polarity and the theological mess that follows is interesting to me because I see it as the beginning of a very important process in the Church's theological history. The issue it addresses is very important, which is this: who does what in the salvific partnership of God/man? Which one starts the salvific process? Who does the most work? I will now give a brief interpretation of this conflict.

Pelagius appeared to have a strong aversion to emphasizing the significance of original sin. In the context of the nature/nurture schism, it could be said that Pelagius was working with more nurture-oriented, existential, humanistic presuppositions. While some heresy-hunters are quick to accuse Pelagius of minimizing the need for grace, I think he simply thought of grace differently. Grace to Pelagius is free will, an individual conscience and reason. He embodied the milieu of the now Eastern Church in his emphasis of free will and speculative humanism. In this context, Pelagian soteriology revolves around the idea that man can initiate the restoration process that we call salvation.

Regarding Augustine, I see him as the soteriological poster-child of the Western Church. Augustine is perhaps *too* logical in developing his doctrines – to the point of deviating from scripture as the theological matrix. Rather, many of his ideas (such as his personal predestination) were developed in a logical way that he felt must be Biblical. Note that for Augustine, it is logic before exegesis. And because of this, Augustinian soteriology revolves around the idea that only God can initiate the salvific restoration process. For several years, these two theologians play the main soteriological roles in the story that the Church finds itself in. And it is in the midst of their thesis/antithesis overcorrectional volley that we have derived most of our soteriology.

I do not have a large amount of respect for many of the main soteriological theologians who follow these two. Most of them suffer from what I think of as the *Beza Complex*. This philosophical crutch that is so frequently employed by contemporary thinkers is marked by a person who ideologically edits someone else's work rather than conceiving of their own original idea or theory. This process usually carries the original idea to "logical" extremes or conclusions that were never intended by the original thinker, i.e. the continental philosophers, partially-educated contemporary theologians, and, of course, Beza.

As we reflect upon how the many great theologians of the past have put forth so much effort in describing how we are saved, I think we should observe a complication that arises in approaching soteriology as such a science. I find that we can interpret the grounds of our own salvation – as well as someone else's – however we like. And the most frightening part about this is how we can find scriptures to backup Pelagian and Augustinian approaches. If I want to think of my salvation as determined by God, I can emotionally, rationally, and scripturally convince myself that this is the case in the same way that I can fully persuade myself that I am the author of my salvation. As is always the case when interpreting deterministic issues, we are in danger of molding reality to our paradigms. And because the only concrete examples we can use when dealing with deterministic issues are in retrospect, we can usually satisfactorily reinterpret our experiences according to whatever theory we want to explore. The result parallels Odysseus's encounter with the demented innkeeper: this innkeeper only had one bed, and if the customer was too tall to fit, the innkeeper would "shorten" the man to fit the bed. Likewise, if the customer was too short, he would be stretched to suitably fit. I must say that I see this pattern in many theologians chopping and stretching salvific reality to fit their soteriological bed.

My conclusion should be (by this time) remotely predictable: in light of how much liberty we can take in subjectively interpreting an already subjective reality, I think it is best that we admit to not being exactly sure how we are saved and rather focus on continually working out our salvation. It sickens me how there has been so much bloodshed within the Church over these issues. When will we abandon our modernistic urge to always construct a binary, conclusive, dogmatic taxonomy when doing theological reflection? If we can abstain from this mind frame when formulating our soteriology, we will begin to notice a more *dharmic* ideal of what it means to have the image and likeness of God restored within humanity. And when this is the case, I believe we will find 5-point Calvinists and Armenians humbled together before the freedom we can find in embracing this salvific enigma. Hey, I can dream can't I?

IV SANCTIFICATION

"I have heard what the talkers are talking,
and there will never be more perfection than there now is."
-Walt Whitman

"There is no justification without sanctification, no forgiveness without renewal of life,
no real faith from which the fruits of new obedience do not grow."
-Martin Luther

I remember at the age of 8 reading the first chapters of Genesis in my picture Bible. I got to the part where Cain was getting jealous of the other guy and God came to speak with him about it. I will never forget reading the part where God told Cain, "Sin is crouching at your door, but you can master it." It was the first time the possibility occurred to me that we might not always *have* to sin. Although I never really looked farther into it, I kept the issue somewhere in the back of my head. I never would have guessed that so many people made such a big deal out of it. Can we obey? Do we have to perpetually struggle with sin in some degree? Can we ever really please God?

Wesleyan Perfection

Many Church traditions have some kind of sanctification theology. Wesleyans have a doctrine that they affectionately call *entire sanctification* or *Christian perfection*. The essence of this doctrine is faith in the justifying power of Christ's blood that is expressed in a pure love for God and man. The recurring theme of Christian perfection is to love the Lord you God with all your heart, soul, mind, and strength and to love your neighbor as yourself. In this view, the total and consuming love of God (and thus man) is thought of as the prevailing constant of the Law. The greatest misconception that people tend to have with Wesley's presentation of his ideals is in thinking that this sanctification allows us to fulfill the Law. We error in thinking that we are sanctified from sins of infirmity. Wesley addresses this by explaining that sins of infirmity refer to the violation of the Law, and because we are no longer under the Law, we are no longer charged with sin whenever we inadvertently break it. The perfection that this sanctification allows is a perfection of intention and love, not of legal flawlessness.

Wesley maintained that salvation is extended to the "entire work of God," from the gentlest nudges of conscience to the searing convictions of the Spirit. He further breaks his salvific concept down into two broad parts: *justification* and *sanctification*.

He defines justification in terms of the forgiveness of sins (and the implicational reacceptance with God that accompanies it). This justification brings with it peace, hope, and joy. After the initial experience of this justification, the believer is prone to think that all sin has been removed and destroyed from their life completely and permanently; but this is a common misconception that is usually the first of a long struggle between the flesh and the spirit. He strongly points out that it is important to note that we must understand the fact that we are forgiven and restored before we can have a true assurance of faith in our justification.

Wesley also firmly asserts that faith is the one and true condition of our justification (I believe we may use his term "justification" and "conversion" interchangeably). He sums this up in a statement that basically says no person can ever be justified without first believing; and in the same way any person who believes in the justifying work of Christ *is* justified. However he is also quick to mention the role of repentance in our justification. The works that are appropriately associated with repentance have their place in our faith, but these works are not constitutional as we often misunderstand them to be. Wesley describes sanctification in the same regard by maintaining that faith is the avenue of our salvation.

This doctrine has had a very hard life, mostly do to linguistic ambiguities. Wesley's usage of the Biblical word "perfect" is substantially disturbing to some, but we must continually remind ourselves that the perfection he speaks of is a *perfection of intention*, not the flawless, inerrant fulfillment of the law. The language Wesleyans use in speaking of Christian perfection refers to a complete, sincere and total love for God and man.

In this mind-frame, can we become "sinless?" If we do not call sins of infirmity "sins," but rather "mistakes" (as he does), then yes, we can become sinless. But it is with these terms that we must be careful. I can pardon a mistake that emerges from a "perfected" saint, but a mortal sin should not come from him in the way it did before his sanctification. But we are not addressing mistakes. I have no problem if Christ forgot someone's name or accidentally sneezed near the High Priest. But if he hit his hand with a hammer, what would have come out of his mouth? What if his hand was hit with a nail?

Ever since I read the story of Cain and Abel I have believed that we do not need to be in bondage to habitual sin after we are justified before God. I simply believe that if God requires obedience – whether it is regarding keeping the Sabbath or keeping a pure heart – He will enable us to fulfill that standard. Sometimes, even in regard to sins of infirmity, I simply cannot bring myself to say that Christ's blood isn't strong enough to completely free us.

The kind of obedience/sanctification that I am referring to is just as much a part of salvation as our initial justification is. Wesley does a wonderful job emphasizing this, and I believe there is merit in the Biblical teachings that he articulates, even if I am troubled by his language. Regardless, the ideal of salvation that he describes is the type of dynamic process that I hope the evangelical enterprise soon recognizes as truly life abundant.

CONCLUSION

As we reflect upon the reality of salvation, I hope that we are continually over-whelmed by the grandeur of this beautiful mystery. The questions that we so often raise from Genesis, Romans, Galatians, etc often change who we are by simply asking them. I am altogether ok with the idea that we may never have conclusive answers to the details of justification, the ego or the origin of sin. But I am not egocentric enough to assume this attitude is for everyone. However, I must reemphasize the ethos of my credo to be this: regarding salvation, I believe we are wiser for suspending judgment on such ideas as these that are as lofty as they are important. Never stop seeking; but perhaps the wisest spiritual advice I have ever received was to *learn to enjoy the seeking*. Learn to enjoy the mystery.

To close, let us review some of the more important areas of reflection. What does it mean to work out one's salvation? There are several important implications that can be gathered from how one attempts to answer this question, and I encourage the reader to pause and reflect upon each:

1. Am I working out my salvation or have I attained it?
2. What part of my being is able to be restored?
3. How much do I think I have to know about God to be saved?
4. Is the point of God's work on Earth to enable us to go to Heaven?
5. Is it impossible to overcome sin?
6. Are we completely incapable of pursuing God?
7. In light of this understanding of salvation, what is damnation?
8. What would cause one to be damned?
   and lastly,
9. Why has God chosen to renew us?

In the midst of my skepticism and confusion, I view every day that I wake up as an opportunity to work out my salvation. As I run, I contemplate it. Salvation. Arahat-ship. Moksha. Enlightenment. So many words to describe the same goal. Peoples of faith have tried to employ many different approaches to achieve it. Whatever your under-standing of salvation is, I hope you can pull something out of this paper that encourages you to work it out every day, with fear and trembling. With doubt and angst. With late nights and long walks. With prayer and study. With pain. With joy. With reason. With people. Introspection. Sunsets. Sacraments. Tradition. Jogs. And long-winded papers filled with too much convoluted circumlocution and philosophic speculation.

Bibliography

Barth, Karl. *Church Dogmatics, Volume III: The Doctrine of Creation, Part 1*, T & T Clark Ltd, Edinburgh, Scotland, 1958.

Berkhof, Louis. *Systematic Theology*, Fourth Edition, Grand Rapids: Eerdmans, 1939.

Bonhoeffer, Dietrich. *Dietrich Bonhoeffer Works, Volume 3: Creation and Fall*, Fortress Press, Minneapolis, Minnesota, 1997.

Grenz, Stanley. *Theology for the Community of God*, Broadman & Holman Publishers, Nashville Tennessee, 1994.

Grudem, Wayne. *Systematic Theology*, Inter-Varsity Press, Zondervan Publishing House, Grand Rapids, Michigan, 1994.

Landis, Robert W. *The Immortality of the Soul*, Fourth Edition, Carlton & Porter, New York, NY, 1859.